Walking bass studies
for Baritone ukulele

Ondřej Šárek

Contents

On the cover there is my son's Antonín (8) picture called „ Guinea pig at the cottage".

Introduction

In this book you will find ten pieces on which you can practice walking bass on the ukulele. I chose a well-known jazz chord progression. In addition to the walking bass, I also added melodies.

A few notes on playing songs.
Maintain a dynamic difference between melody and bass. It can help if you play the bass with your thumb and the melody with the other fingers.
Start at a slow pace. And when you master the song, speed it up

Here is a link to a youtube demo in the study music tempo: https://youtu.be/dJO3wRXmgL0

How to read tablature

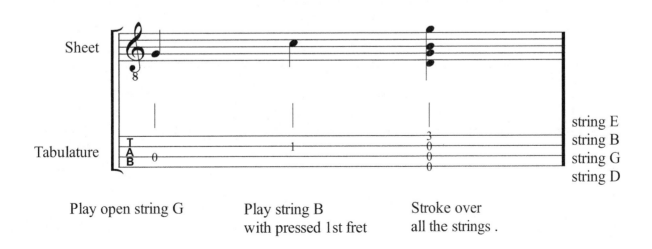

Play open string G   Play string B   Stroke over
         with pressed 1st fret all the strings .

I.

Ondřej Šárek

I.

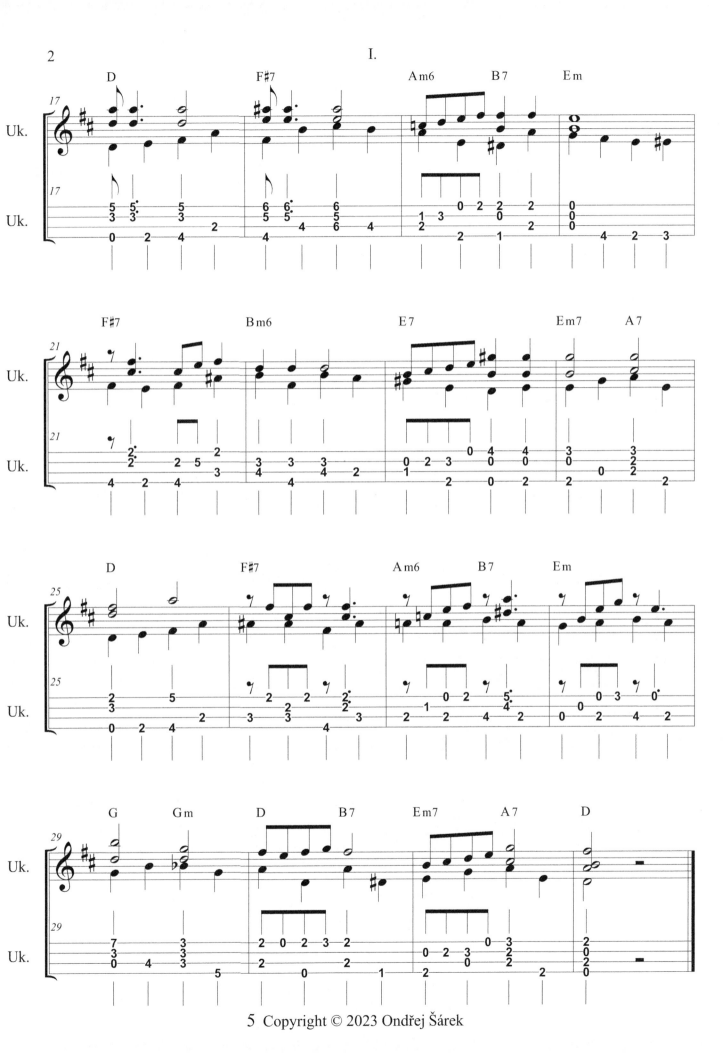

II.

Ondřej Šárek

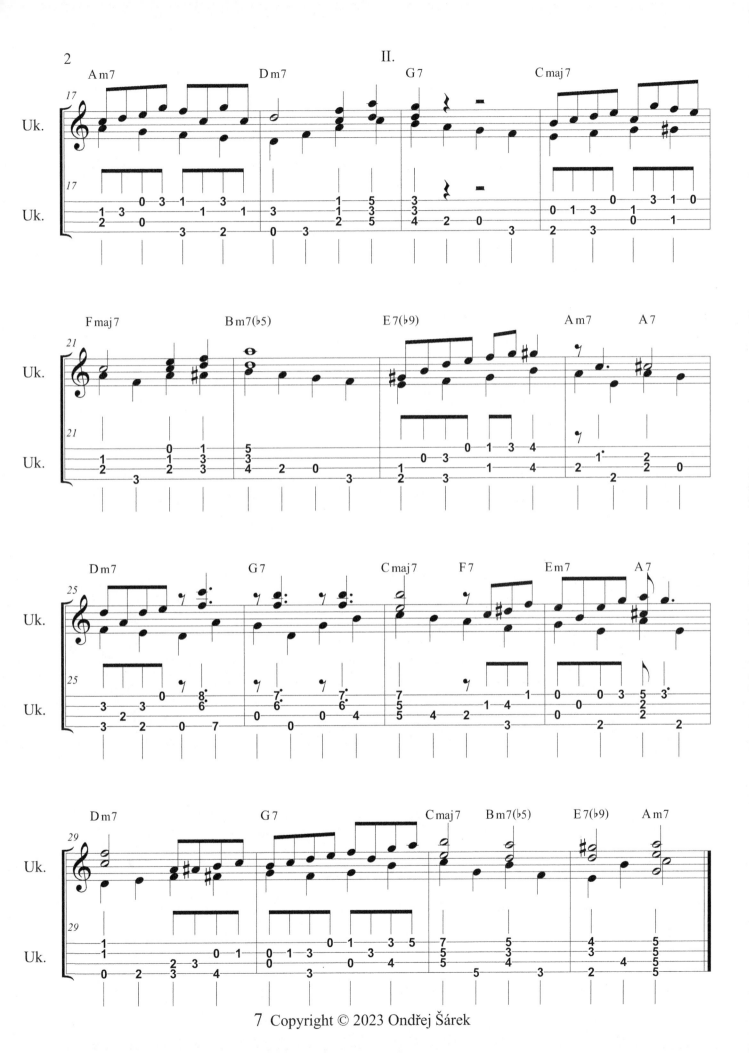

2

II.

III.

Ondřej Šárek

III.

IV.

Ondřej Šárek

IV.

V.

Ondřej Šárek

VI.

Ondřej Šárek

VI.

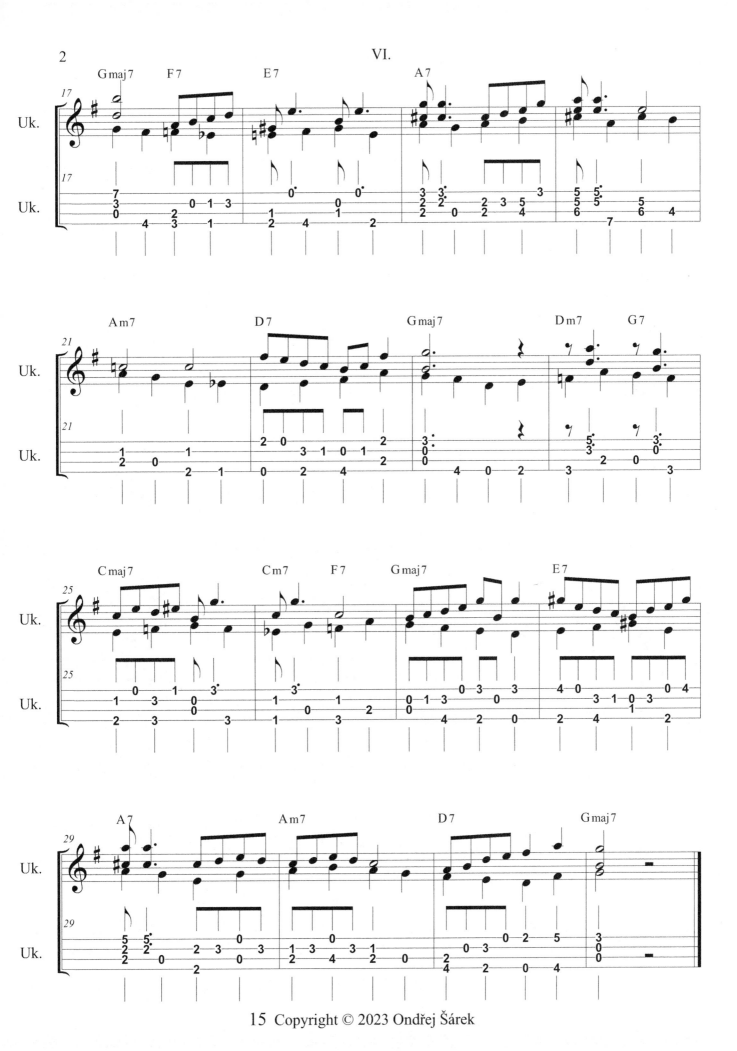

VII.

Ondřej Šárek

VII.

VIII.

Ondřej Šárek

2

VIII.

IX.

Ondřej Šárek

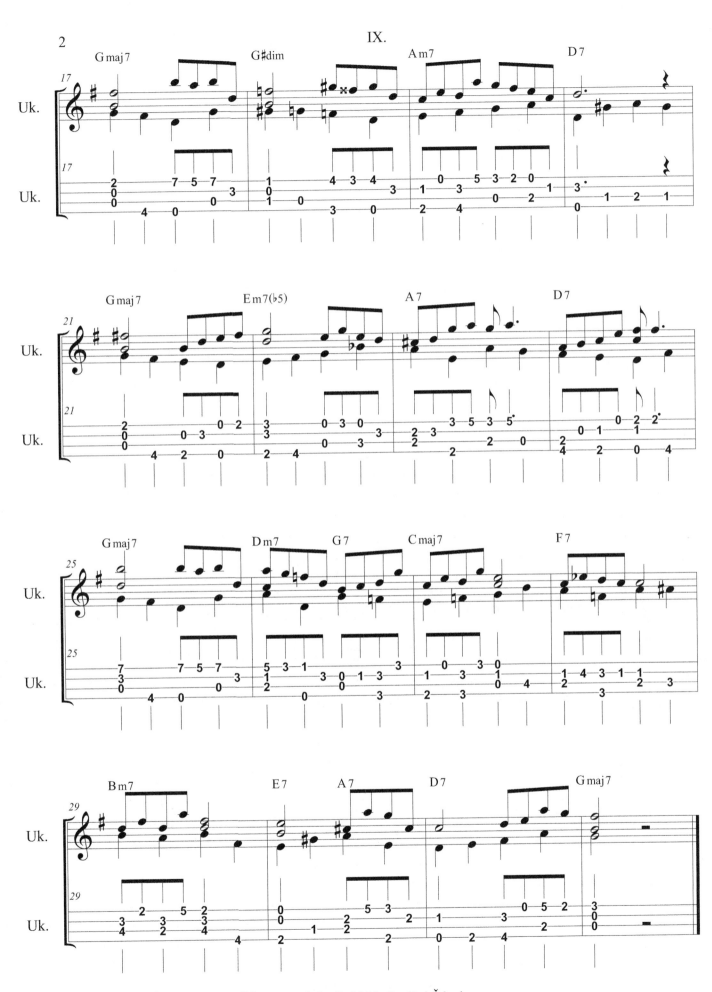

X.

Ondřej Šárek

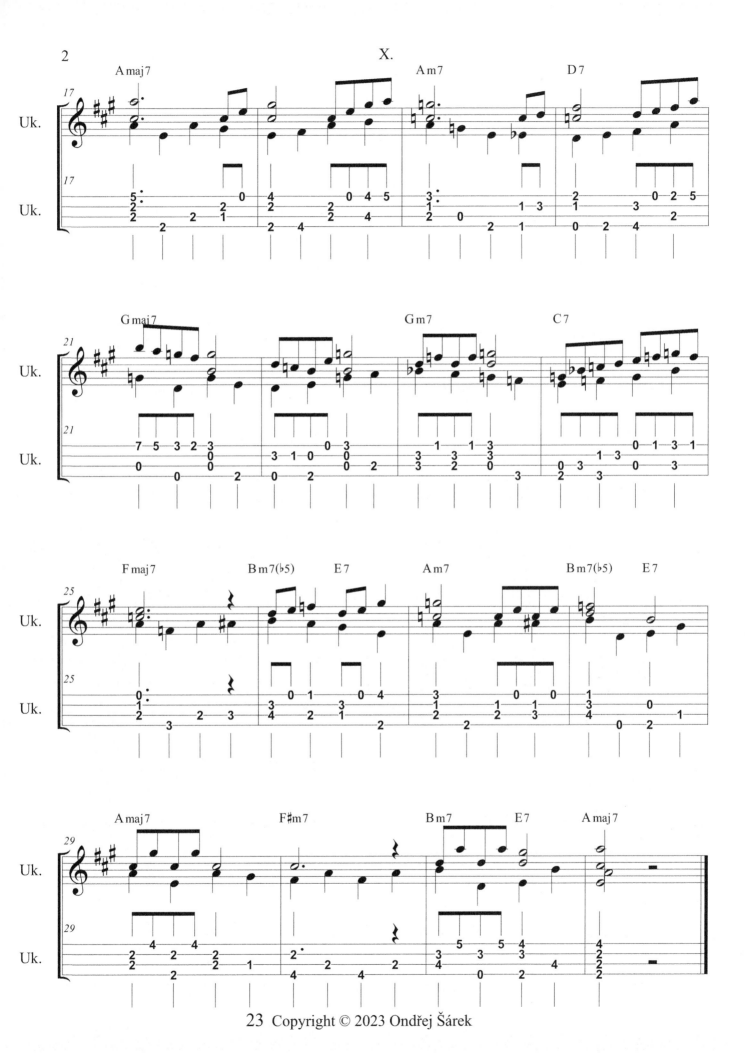

For C tuning ukulele
Classics for Ukulele (MB)
Ukulele Bluegrass Solos (MB)
Antonin Dvorak: Biblical Songs
Irish tunes for all ukulele
Gospel Ukulele Solos
Gregorian chant for Ukulele
The Czech Lute for Ukulele
Romantic Pieces by Frantisek Max Knize for Ukulele
Notebook for Anna Magdalena Bach and Ukulele
Open Tunings for Ukulel (MB)
Robert Burns songs for ukulele
Jewish songs for C tuning ukulele
Campanella style songbook for beginner
Antonín Dvořák: opera The Jacobin for ukulele
Leopold Mozart's Notebook for Wolfgang Arranged for Ukulele (MB)
The canons for one or two ukuleles
Solo and Variations for ukulele volume 1., 2., 3.
Czech Medieval Ukulele
Christmas Carols for ukulele
Harmonics for ukulele
43 Ghiribizzi by Niccolo Paganini for Ukulele
Christmas Carols for Clawhammer ukulele
Gospel Clawhammer ukulele Solos
Czech Renaissance folk songs for Ukulele
Classical music for Clawhammer Ukulele
Christmas Carols for Crosspicking Ukulele
Josef Pekárek Two Hanakian operas for Ukulele
How to play on three ukulele simultaneously
Clawhammer solo for Ukulele
Gospel Crosspicking Ukulele Solos
48 Fingerstyle Studies for Ukulele
Compositions for ukulele
18 Dance Tunes from Caslav Region for Ukulele
Francisco Tárrega for Ukulele (MB)
10 songs from the years 1899-1920 for Ukulele
Czech Hymnbook for Ukulele
Campanella style songbook for intermediate
Songs from old Prague for Ukulele
Lute music by Nicolaus Schmall von Lebendorf for Ukulele
15 Japanese Songs for Ukulele
Interesting Moravian songs for Ukulele
Bohemian Zwiefacher for Ukulele
Ludwig van Beethoven Dances for Ukulele
Carols from the world for Ukulele
Slovak songs for Ukulele
Songs from the Czech National Revival for Ukulele
Tyrolean songs for Ukulele
Pentatonic scales exercises for ukulele
Single String Melodies for Ukulele
Open Tunings songbook for Ukulele
Czech Hymnbook for campanella style Ukulele
12 Walzer by Vojtech Jirovec for Ukulele
12 Krönungsintraden by J. I. Linek for Ukulele
Trutznachtigall - Baroque Songs by Friedrich Spee for Ukulele
24 Horn Duets for solo Ukulele
Polish folk song for Ukulele
Irish tunes for beginner on ukulele
Folk songs from Brno for Ukulele

For C tuning with low G
Irish tunes for all ukulele
Gospel Ukulele low G Solos
Antonin Dvorak: Biblical Songs: for Ukulele with low G
Gregorian chant for Ukulele with low G
The Czech Lute for Ukulele with low G
Romantic Pieces by Frantisek Max Knize for Ukulele with low G
Notebook for Anna Magdalena Bach and Ukulele with low G
Robert Burns songs for ukulele with low G
Jewish songs for ukulele with low G
Campanella style songbook for beginner: ukulele with low G
Czech Medieval Ukulele with low G
Christmas Carols for ukulele with low G
Fingerpicking solo for Ukulele with low G
43 Ghiribizzi by Niccolo Paganini for Ukulele with low G
Christmas Carols for Crosspicking Ukulele with low G
Czech Renaissance folk songs for Ukulele with low G
Gospel Crosspicking Ukulele with low G Solos
Josef Pekárek Two Hanakian operas for Ukulele with low G
18 Dance Tunes from Caslav Region for Ukulele with low G
10 songs from the years 1899-1920 for Ukulele with low G
Czech Hymnbook for Ukulele with low G
Boogie woogie patterns for ukulele with low G
Compositions for ukulele with low G
Second Fingerpicking solo for Ukulele with low G
Double Stop Gospel for Ukulele with low G
Songs from old Prague for Ukulele with low G
Lute music by Nicolaus Schmall von Lebendorf for Ukulele with low G
15 Japanese Songs for Ukulele with low G
Interesting Moravian songs for Ukulele with low G
Bohemian Zwiefacher for Ukulele with low G
12 Krönungsintraden by J. I. Linek for Ukulele with low G
Ludwig van Beethoven Dances for Ukulele with low G
Carols from the world for Ukulele with low G
Slovak songs for Ukulele with low G
16 Studies for Ukulele with Low G on Bass Strings
Songs from the Czech National Revival for Ukulele with low G
Tyrolean songs for Ukulele with low G
Single String Melodies for Ukulele with Low G
Pentatonic scales exercises for Ukulele with low G
12 Walzer by Vojtech Jirovec for Ukulele with low G
Polish folk song for Ukulele with low G
Trutznachtigall - Baroque Songs by Friedrich Spee for Ukulele with low G
24 Horn Duets for solo Ukulele with Low G
Folk songs from Brno for Ukulele with low G
Walking bass studies for Ukulele with Low G

For Baritone ukulele
Irish tunes for all ukulele
Gospel Baritone Ukulele Solos
Antonin Dvorak: Biblical Songs: for Baritone Ukulele
Gregorian chant for Baritone Ukulele
The Czech Lute for Baritone Ukulele
Romantic Pieces by Frantisek Max Knize for Baritone Ukulele
Notebook for Anna Magdalena Bach and Baritone Ukulele
Robert Burns songs for Baritone ukulele
Jewish songs for baritone ukulele
Campanella style songbook for beginner: Baritone ukulele
Czech Medieval Baritone Ukulele
Christmas Carols for Baritone ukulele
Fingerpicking solo for Baritone ukulele
43 Ghiribizzi by Niccolo Paganini for Baritone ukulele
Christmas Carols for Crosspicking Baritone ukulele

Czech Renaissance folk songs for Baritone ukulele
Gospel Crosspicking Baritone Ukulele Solos
Josef Pekárek Two Hanakian operas for Baritone Ukulele
18 Dance Tunes from Caslav Region for Baritone Ukulele
10 songs from the years 1899-1920 for Baritone Ukulele
Czech Hymnbook for Baritone Ukulele
Boogie woogie patterns for Baritone Ukulele
Compositions for Baritone Ukulele
Second Fingerpicking solo for Baritone Ukulele
Double Stop Gospel for Baritone Ukulele
Songs from old Prague for Baritone Ukulele
Lute music by Nicolaus Schmall von Lebendorf for Baritone Ukulele
15 Japanese Songs for Baritone Ukulele
Bohemian Zwiefacher for Baritone ukulele
Interesting Moravian songs for Baritone ukulele
12 Krönungsintraden by J. I. Linek for Baritone Ukulele
Ludwig van Beethoven Dances for Baritone Ukulele
Carols from the world for Baritone Ukulele
Bitonality Songbook for Baritone Ukulele
Slovak songs for Baritone ukulele
16 Studies for Baritone ukulele on Bass Strings
Songs from the Czech National Revival for Baritone Ukulele
Tyrolean songs for Baritone Ukulele
Single String Melodies for Baritone Ukulele
Pentatonic scales exercises for Baritone Ukulele
12 Walzer by Vojtech Jirovec for Baritone ukulele
Polish folk song for Baritone ukulele
Trutznachtigall - Baroque Songs by Friedrich Spee for Baritone Ukulele
24 Horn Duets for solo Baritone ukulele
Folk songs from Brno for Baritone Ukulele
Walking bass studies for Baritone ukulele

For Cuatro Tuning Ukulele (g3-c4-e4-a3)
Gospel for Cuatro Tuning Ukulele
10 songs from the years 1899-1920 for Cuatro Tuning Ukulele
Bohemian Zwiefacher for Cuatro Tuning Ukulele
Classical music for Cuatro Tuning Ukulele
Carols from the world for Cuatro Tuning Ukulele

For D tuning ukulele
Skola hry na ukulele (G+W s.r.o.)
Irish tunes for all ukulele
Jewish songs for D tuning ukulele
Campanella style songbook for beginner: D tuning ukulele

For EADA tuning ukulele
EADA ukulele tuning
Gospel EADA Ukulele Solos

For Baritone ukulele with high D
Jewish songs for baritone ukulele with high D
Campanella style songbook for beginner: Baritone ukulele with high D
Solo and Variations for Baritone ukulele with high D volume 1., 2., 3.

Ukulele Duets
Notebook for Anna Magdalena Bach, C tuning ukulele and C tuning ukulele
Notebook for Anna Magdalena Bach, C tuning ukulele and Ukulele with low G
Notebook for Anna Magdalena Bach, C tuning ukulele and Baritone ukulele
Notebook for Anna Magdalena Bach, Ukulele with low G and Ukulele with low G
Notebook for Anna Magdalena Bach, Ukulele with low G and Baritone ukulele
Notebook for Anna Magdalena Bach, Baritone ukulele and Baritone ukulele
The canons for one or two ukuleles
Mauro Giuliani arranged for Ukulele Duet
Notebook for Anna Magdalena Bach for Ukulele
and EADGBE Guitar
Notebook for Wolfgang for Ukulele and EADGBE Guitar
12 Walzer by Vojtěch Jírovec for two Ukulele
12 Walzer by Vojtěch Jírovec for Ukulele and EADGBE Guitar
12 Krönungsintraden by J.I. Linek for two Ukulele
Gospel for two Ukuleles

Duet for Mandolin and other instrument
Notebook for Anna Magdalena Bach for Mandolin and EADGBE Guitar Notebook for Anna Magdalena Bach for Mandolin and instrument from the mandolin family
Notebook for Wolfgang for Mandolin and EADGBE Guitar
Notebook for Wolfgang for Mandolin and instrument
from the mandolin family

For 6 sting ukulele (Liliʻu ukulele)
Gospel 6 string Ukulele Solos
Gregorian chant for 6 string Ukulele
Notebook for Anna Magdalena Bach and 6 string Ukulele
Robert Burns songs for 6 string ukulele
Songs from old Prague for 6 string Ukulele
Lute music by Nicolaus Schmall
von Lebendorf for 6 string Ukulele
Bohemian Zwiefacher for 6 string Ukulele
Jewish songs for 6 string Ukulele
Carols from the world for 6 string Ukulele
Slovak songs for 6 string Ukulele
Trutznachtigall - Baroque Songs by Friedrich Spee for 6 string Ukulele
Songs from the Czech National Revival for 6 string Ukulele
Polish folk song for 6 string Ukulele
Tyrolean songs for 6 string Ukulele

For Slide ukulele (lap steel ukulele)
Comprehensive Slide Ukulele: Guidance for Slide Ukulele Playing
Gospel Slide Ukulele Solos
Irish tunes for slide ukulele
Robert Burns songs for Slide ukulele

Open G Baritone Ukulele or 5-string banjo (dgbd)
Gospel for Open G Baritone Ukulele or 5-string banjo
Jewish songs for Open G Baritone Ukulele or 5-string banjo
Robert Burns songs for Open G Baritone Ukulele or 5-string banjo

Cavaquinho Portugues (cgad)
Carols from the world for Cavaquinho Portugues
Gospel for Cavaquinho Portugues
Slovak songs for Cavaquinho Portugues
18 popular Czech Minuet for Cavaquinho Portugues
10 songs from the years 1899-1920 for Cavaquinho Portugues

Songs from old Prague for Cavaquinho Portugues
Folk songs from Brno for Cavaquinho Portugues
Polish folk song for Cavaquinho Portugues
Lute music by Nicolaus Schmall von Lebendorf for Cavaquinho Portugues

Cavaquinho Portugues (ggbd)
Carols from the world for Cavaquinho Portugues
Gospel for Cavaquinho Portugues
Classical music for Cavaquinho Portugues
Lute music by Nicolaus Schmall von Lebendorf for Cavaquinho Portugues
Songs from old Prague for Cavaquinho Portugues
18 popular Czech Minuet for Cavaquinho Portugues
Slovak songs for Cavaquinho Portugues
10 songs from the years 1899-1920 for Cavaquinho Portugues

Polish folk song for Cavaquinho Portugues
Folk songs from Brno for Cavaquinho Portugues
Tyrolean songs for Ukulele for Cavaquinho Portugues

Timple Canario
Carols from the world for Timple Canario
Campanella style songbook for beginner Timple Canario
Lute music by Nicolaus Schmall von Lebendorf for Timple Canario
Tyrolean songs for Timple Canario
18 popular Czech Minuet for Timple Canario
18 Dance Tunes from Caslav Region for Timple Canario
15 Japanese Songs for Timple Canario
Slovak songs for Timple Canario
Ludwig van Beethoven Dances for Timple Canario
12 Krönungsintraden by J. I. Linek for Timple Canario
Polish folk song for Timple Canario
Songs from old Prague for Timple Canario
Songs from the Czech National Revival for Timple Canario
The canons for Timple Canario
Gospel for Timple Canario
Trutznachtigall - Baroque Songs by Friedrich Spee for Timple Canario
24 Horn Duets for solo Timple Canario
10 songs from the years 1899-1920 for Timple Canario
Bohemian Zwiefacher for Timple Canario
Folk songs from Brno for Timple Canario
Gregorian chant for Timple Canario
Notebook for Anna Magdalena Bach and Timple Canario
Jewish songs for Timple Canario

Tres Cubano traditionally tuned g4 g3 - c4 c4 - e4 e3
Gospel for Tres Cubano
Songbooks for Tres Cubano volume 1., 2.
Jewish songs for Tres Cubano

Tres Cubano (split-string stroke) traditionally tuned g4 g3 - c4 c4 - e4 e3
Tres Cubano Big Songbook
Gregorian chant for Tres Cubano
Songs from old Prague for Tres Cubano
Carols from the world for Tres Cubano
Lute music by Nicolaus Schmall von Lebendorf for Tres Cubano
15 Japanese Folk Songs for Tres Cubano
Notebook for Anna Magdalena Bach and Tres Cubano
Bohemian Zwiefacher for Tres Cubano
Slovak songs for Tres Cubano
Tyrolean songs for Tres Cubano
Classical music for Tres Cubano
10 songs from the years 1899-1920 for Tres Cubano

Tres Cubano Modern tuning: g4 g3 c4 c4 e4 e4
Gospel for Tres Cubano
Jewish songs for Tres Cubano
Songs from the Czech National Revival for Tres Cubano
Carols from the world for Tres Cubano
18 popular Czech Minuet for Tres Cubano
Slovak songs for Tres Cubano
Tyrolean songs for Tres Cubano
18 Dance Tunes from Caslav Region for Tres Cubano
12 Krönungsintraden by J. I. Linek for Tres Cubano
Trutznachtigall - Baroque Songs by Friedrich Spee for Tres Cubano
The Czech Lute for Tres Cubano
Polish folk song for Tres Cubano
Czech Hymnbook for Tres Cubano

Kalimba

Songbook for Kalimba B11 Melody
Second songbook for Kalimba B11 Melody
Songbooks for Kalimba Am+G
Czech Hymnbook for Alto *Hugh Tracey* Kalimba
Robert Burns songs for Alto *Hugh Tracey* Kalimba
Songbooks for Kalimba E116
Songbooks for Alto *Hugh Tracey* Kalimba
Songbooks for Kalimba *Heavenly A tuning*
First Songbooks for 10 Key Kalimba
Second Songbooks for 10 Key Kalimba
Gregorian chant for Alto *Hugh Tracey* Kalimba
Gospel songs for Alto *Hugh Tracey* Kalimba
Jewish songs for Alto *Hugh Tracey* Kalimba
Songbooks for Kalimba C diatonic tuning
Irish tunes for Alto Hugh Tracey Kalimba
12 Japanese Folk Songs for Alto Hugh Tracey Kalimba
Bohemian Zwiefacher and Minet for Alto Hugh Tracey Kalimba
Carols from the world for Alto Hugh Tracey Kalimba
Tyrolean songs for Alto Hugh Tracey Kalimba
Carols from the world for C major 17 Key Kalimba
12 Japanese Folk Songs for C major 17 Key Kalimba
Jewish songs for C major 17 Key Kalimba
Songbooks for C major 17 Key Kalimba
Czech Hymnbook for C major 17 Key Kalimba
Robert Burns songs for C major 17 Key Kalimba
Lidovky a koledy pro kalimbu 1.díl
Songbooks for C major 8 Key Kalimba
Tyrolean songs for C major 17 Key Kalimba
Gospel songs for C major 17 Key Kalimba
Carols from the world for 34 Key Chromatic Kalimba

Diatonic Accordion (Melodeon) books

For G/C diatonic accordion

Bass songbook for G/C melodeon
Cross row style songbook for beginner
G/C diatonic accordion
Gospel G/C diatonic accordion Solos
9 songs from the years 1899-1920 for G/C melodeon
Czech Hymnbook for G/C melodeon
Songbook for G/C diatonic accordion *Volume 1.*
Songbook for G/C diatonic accordion *Volume 2.*
18 popular Czech Minuet for G/C diatonic accordion
Songs from old Prague for G/C diatonic accordion
Classical music for G/C diatonic accordion
Bohemian Zwiefacher for G/C diatonic accordion
Tyrolean songs for G/C diatonic accordion
15 Japanese Folk Songs for G/C diatonic accordion

Slovak songs for G/C diatonic accordion

For C/F diatonic accordion

Cross row style songbook for beginner
C/F diatonic accordion
Gospel C/F diatonic accordion Solos
9 songs from the years 1899-1920 for C/F melodeon
Classical music for C/F diatonic accordion

For D/G diatonic accordion

Cross row style songbook for beginner
D/G diatonic accordion
Gospel D/G diatonic accordion Solos
9 songs from the years 1899-1920 for D/G melodeon
Classical music for D/G diatonic accordion

Anglo Concertina books

For C/G 30-button Wheatstone

Lachenal System

Gospel Anglo Concertina Solos
Notebook for Anna Magdalena Bach and Anglo Concertina

Robert Burns songs for Anglo Concertina
The Czech Lute for Anglo Concertina
Gregorian chant for Anglo Concertina
Josef Pekárek *Two Hanakian operas* for Anglo Concertina

For C/G 20-button

Gospel C/G Anglo Concertina Solos
Robert Burns songs for C/G Anglo Concertina
Gregorian chant for Anglo Concertina

New Flute Recorder books

18 Dance Tunes from Caslav Region for Recorder Quartet
Josef Pekárek Two Hanakian operas for Recorder Quartet
Czech Medieval Songs For Two Recorders
Robert Burns songs for Recorder Quartet
Songs from old Prague for Recorder Quartet
15 Japanese Folk Songs for Recorder Quartet

Saxophone Quartet books

18 Dance Tunes from Caslav Region for Saxophone Quartet
Josef Pekárek Two Hanakian operas for Saxophone Quartet
Robert Burns songs for Saxophone Quartet
Songs from old Prague for Saxophone Quartet

Printed in Great Britain
by Amazon

47065383R00020